JOY IN THE MAKING

By the same author:

Fun and Games with Shropshire Names

Joy in the Making

by

Monica Bott

(Derivation: Robert Bridges;
"I love all beauteous things")

BREWIN BOOKS

First published
by Brewin Books, Studley, Warwickshire. B80 7LG
in April 1991

ISBN 0 947731 87 3

Typeset in Baskerville 11pt.
and made and printed in Great Britain by
Supaprint (Redditch) Ltd.

ABOUT THE AUTHOR

Monica Bott is a writer and watercolour painter who has lived in Church Stretton all her life. Her latest book "Joy in the Making" is a series of twelve essays, mainly devoted to Shropshire, and illustrated with reproductions of the artist's own watercolours.

"OVER THE LONGMYND"
(see page 60)

CONTENTS

LIST OF ILLUSTRATIONS

All the following illustrations and the cover design are reproductions of original watercolours painted by the author.

"THE COMMISSION"

"I'd like a picture, yes indeed,
If you could do the painting;
A bit of colour, something bright,
Is just what I be wanting . . . . .

It needn't be a large one, now,
And nothing complicated;
There's some as cover half the wall,
I think they're over-rated . . . . .

And as for them queer modern things,
With dabs of this and that;
They bother me, for I can't tell
What they be striving at . . . . .

I wouldn't want a portrait, no,
They sometimes look quite tearful;
And we girls wasn't much for looks;
No - give me something cheerful . . . . .

Of course, a view looks very well,
Seems suitable, and proper;
With fancy frame, and mount - and then
As like as not, I'd drop her . . . . .

I think p'rhaps flowers would be the best,
And finish with this fretting;
Seems silly, though, when just outside,
There's masses for the getting . . . . .

I want a picture, yes indeed,
It's kind of you to do it;
But choosing's hard, and I don't know -
I think I'll leave you to it."

"CHELMICK"

"CHELMICK"

I remember the cottage since schooldays, cunningly hidden in a fold of the Stretton hills. How often, after a long walk, we would turn thankfully down the steep winding lane, past the farm and the duckpond, (always it seemed, lively with a young family of fluffy ducklings in those days.) Then, where the gradient eased and the lane curved again, there was a little white gate affording the only glimpse, through thick holly hedges, of a stone-flagged path, bordered with trees and flowers and a curve of thatch on stone walls.

How I longed to see what lay beyond, for the front of the cottage was hidden; the roof sloped steeply to the level of the road, without a window. Whatever secrets it held, they were secure from the inquisitive eyes of casual passers-by. In later years I learned that it belonged to a Mr. Jones, who lived there alone, since his wife had died some years before. Gardening was his life and rare and "difficult" plants were his family. The garden was warm and sheltered and the plants grew well for him; he was able to market them and make a modest living. To keen gardeners he was well known and many visitors taking tea at a cottage catering for them not far away, often called to see him to take home carefully some of his garden treasures.

Time eventually defeated Mr. Jones, though not his garden. He is, I think, buried in the churchyard just over the brow of the hill that shelters the ground he tended and culti-vated so well. A cottage and "parcel of land" - a tiny heritage - now desolate and left to others, whose interests were more prosaic and hands less skilled and patient than his. The trees and shrubs grew leggy and tangled, the roses ran riot, and grass grew bold and covered everywhere. Impatient hands scythed it off, but little else was done and all grew together as best they might.

A day came when, searching through the local advertise-ments of property for sale, I read that this well remembered spot was to be offered for sale by auction. It was, to me, a momentous announcement for my feelings ranged from hope to despair. I loved the country there, the sturdy stone of the cottage itself and perhaps the garden and its hidden treasures most of all. But an auction! Country cottages were in great demand; lots of people would hear about it and wish to buy, and my purse was far too slender to stand any competiton.

One thing, at least, presented no difficulty. I could go and see it and discover all that lay beyond the little white gate. It was April when I did so. The long walk over the hills - sandwiches and cool light ale enjoyed on a hedge bank, crumbs to the ducklings on the way down the lane, and at last, lifting the latch of the white gate, I was there.

The stone path led me to a porch of rustic timber, enclosed with glass and neatly thatched and this sheltered the cottage door. The living room was large, with a beamed ceiling, and from a corner of it enclosed stairs led to one large bedroom above. A stone pantry lay behind them, and a long kitchen, opening out again to the garden.

From the two windows of the bedroom I could see, far to the left, the blue ridge of Wenlock Edge, while nearer, the little orchard that adjoined the garden, was a dazzling sheet of daffodils - it seemed impossible to set a foot between them. To the right, the Stretton hills rose steeply, but first a long finger of garden streched towards them and two more gates gave access to the lane and to the meadow land that lay in front of the cottage. But I think, above all else that I remember of that enchanted day, the sight of the golden holly trees moved me most. There were at least ten of them and they formed part of the front boundary hedge. Ten feet tall and closely clipped, they stood like tall golden candles, and in the bright sunlight of that April day, outlined against a clear blue sky, they made a picture I shall long remember.

The sun had gone and it was growing chilly when I climbed the hill on my way back to town and money problems and the dreaded prospect of the auction sale. The next few weeks passed like a feverish dream, peopled with strange figures. A solicitor, gruff but kindly, offered advice; the auctioneers looked sceptical on hearing of my finances; the owner was guarded and aloof - for which I could not blame him. Finally, it was agreed; the solicitor would attend the sale and bid for me; I must also be there.

It was the first property auction I had ever attended. About twenty-five people sat on hard wooden chairs in a small dusty room facing the auctioneer and when we arrived there was only standing room. I shrank into a corner, feeling the stare of many speculative eyes and bowed my head over the sale particulars of another larger property which was being offered first. I listened with mounting horror, the opening bid was quite a high one and the price rose steadily, faltered, and rose again, and yet again. I could not follow the bidding - even the flicker of an eyelid seemed to add another £50. It ended at last; a few people moved, chairs scraped, the tension eased a little - then silence again as the auctioneer took up his stand and began reading the preamble to "Lot 2".

There was a map, with areas marked in red (why?), and others in blue (why ever?) and rights of way and complications about maintenance of water supply from the spring in the valley. These dealt with, his stern tones changed and became quite wooing. The phrases "delightful situation", "a property with character and charm", and "unique opportunity" reduced me to utter misery, fearing I had already lost, and I missed the opening bid. Through a haze I heard - "Six hundred I'm bid - any advance on six hundred? Come now, a unique opportunity . . . . ."

One long minute later the hammer fell, my solicitor prodded me firmly and said, "Congratulations - come with me," and I tried to do so, but the floor was rising and falling beneath me like the sea. I remembered nothing clearly until we were in the street. The sight of the blue sky reminded me of the holly trees - they were mine! And the golden orchard - the apple trees - the roses - the white gates, and - why yes - the cottage was mine, too.

. . . .

In early Spring of the following year, my mother and I spent our first weekend there, to explore and get to know our new property. We also needed a sanctuary, to help us recover from the buffetings of Fate.

The weather was all we could have wished, and in the mild Spring sunshine new life was stirring. Under the budding apple trees drifts of snowdrops nodded everywhere, and gold and purple crocus edged the stone-flagged path, to beautiful effect, while more golden holly trees caught and held the sunlight.

Almost unaware, I found myself sitting beside the path, sketch pad on my knee and paintbox ready to hand. It was a memorable day, and there seemed no better way to express my thanks for so much.

"ON BUYING A COUNTRY COTTAGE"

You have belonged to me a few short weeks;
I have behind me forty years of life,
Empty with yearning; rusty with frustration;
A wanderer, with no true anchorage.

The peace you offer me comes strange, as yet;
This little world has led its' life apart;
Your quiet companionship must fold me close,
Before I dare to claim you for my own.

"NEAR LUDHAM, NORFOLK"

How pleasant it is, having hoped for a long time to visit a particular place, to be actually on the way there.

Norfolk was twelve hours travelling distance by road from my home, and as the motor coach gathered speed through the familiar streets, and away on the first lap of its' journey, I reviewed - not for the first time - my reasons for wanting to go there.

It had all started, years before, at a Sale where I chanced to buy a book by the artist Edward Seago. It contained reproductions of many of his paintings, and the majority were of his native county. I was completely fascinated by the effects of light, water and atmosphere recorded there, and the book conveyed, in words and pictures, a great depth of feeling for that part of the country. Gradually I acquired more of his books, and found the same appealing quality. I read them eagerly, and studied them long and assiduously. Perhaps I could paint like that if I studied them sufficiently hard? How absurd that notion was I soon found out, but the books continued to inspire and delight me. I would go on trying, and perhaps one day I would go to Norfolk, and visit some of those already familiar scenes.

By evening, I was thrilled to see the changed landscape. It could scarcely be called landscape - it was more sky-scape. Majestic cloud formations filled the eye, and the land had become flat and insignificant - a mere horizon line. The long hours' confinement in the coach had reduced me to a soporific state where I could almost believe we were not in a coach at all, but a boat, and were drifting steadily out to sea.

I thought how lovely it was. As the dominance of the sky increased, so the earth, and mankind with it, seemed reduced to more humble proportions. Here was a wonderful tranquility, and I began to understand the unique appeal of this part of the country.

We made landfall - or more properly, we arrived - by 9.30 p.m. in Norwich, and a little dazed at finding myself alone in city streets, I sought the house where I would be staying for the next two weeks.

A few days later, a sunny morning gave promise of settled weather, and I set off happily for those "far away places with strange-sounding names" - Wroxham, Horning,

Potter Heigham and Ludham. The last named was my real objective, but I was tempted to linger on the way, beguiled by the busy scenes at Wroxham; the boatyards, and craft of all kinds sprinkled over the Broad, an ever-changing kaleidoscope of colour and movement. A shake, a turn of the head, and all was different. The cabin cruisers were now red, green or white where minutes before there were blue, yellow and grey ones; three white-sailed yachts had suddenly disappeared and a little red-sailed one tacked across importantly in the breeze. Houseboats moored at the water's edge bobbed uncertainly in the wash from moving craft, and reflections everywhere trembled in the ruffled water. It was very captivating, and I longed to stay and watch it all, but today my plans were made, and I would not be diverted.

And so, on to Horning, a main centre for a holiday on the Broads. A picturesque spot, with charming holiday bungalows and chalets built alongside the waterways. Many were thatched, with little gardens and flowering shrubs around them, but although pleasing to look at, it was an artificially contrived landscape, too obviously "pretty" from a painting point of view. It depended, I mused, on what one wanted. Had I been seeking a holiday home, with facilities for boating, or just lazing in the sun, then surely this would be the perfect answer.

"NEAR LUDHAM, NORFOLK"

8

I found my way back to the road, and climbed deter-
minedly on a bus labelled "Ludham" in large letters on the
front. And a quarter of an hour later, I was there.

Almost at once I felt relaxed and at home. Several
roads meandered off in different directions. There were a
few shops; one with the comforting legend "Teas" in the
window. I discovered the way to the Church, a surprisingly
large and impressive one, and as my being there was in the
nature of a pilgrimage, it was fitting that I should go and see
it. As always, however, time was running away with the day,
and I wanted so much to try a sketch somewhere here, and as
usual could not make up my mind where or what it should
be.

I chose another lane, which soon led me away from the
village and into rough meadowland, threaded with dykes
which, strangely, appeared to be above the level of the
surrounding land.

After roaming around for a while, I saw in the distance
a small building, perhaps a boathouse, half hidden by a few
poplar trees. These were possibilities for a picture, so
making my way a little nearer, I unfolded my canvas stool
and sat down to survey the scene. And shortly after that the
comedy began.

Let me confess that my knowledge of yachts and
yachting is painfully small. From the safety of the shore I
have admired their sweeping, graceful lines, as they rise and
dip on the water. There is also that spectacular moment
when the crew (at their peril, it seems) lean over backwards
to a horizontal position, apparently only kept on board by
their toes and a slender bit of the rigging. It is enthralling
to watch - from the shore.

And here I was, in a green meadow, with white yachts
sailing through it at the speed of express trains.

I had started my sketch with the boathouse and the
poplars, and the shining curve of the dyke, but the view was
not complete without a yacht in full sail. The trouble was, I
couldn't catch one.

The first was gone before I was fully aware of its'
presence, but another was just rounding the bend. I started
to draw it, just *there* on the curve, but when I looked up
again, it was nearly out of sight. Numbers 3 and 4 were
equally disobliging. Very well, I would memorise the next
one, and then draw it at my leisure. Here it came, and I
studied it piercingly while it scudded past. Now, as it had
come round the bend, had the foresail been on the left, or
the right, or invisible. I *thought* it was on the left. Wait -
here came another. I watched intently - it was on the right.

I started to draw it, and was shaken to find Number 7 was emphatically on the left. The place must be bewitched, I thought, or had I been sitting in the sun too long?

The explanation of course, was simple. It depended how far round the curve the yacht was when I looked at it, and this presumably depended on the wind; some took a wider curve than others, and once turned and coming nearer, the foresail was on the right.

Once I had captured my yacht, all was well with the world. The hours slipped treacherously away, and all too soon it was bus time.

I walked back over the marshy fields into the lane, my paint bag swinging from side to side.

> "I too, will something make
> And joy in the making;
> Altho' tomorrow it seem
> Like the empty words of a dream,
> Remembered on waking." (*)

Perhaps there lies the key to my mixed feelings of happiness and frustration.

Three men and a dog were coming along the lane. The dog ran over to me, barking excitedly, and I paused to talk to and pat it.

"It's all right, she won't hurt you" called her owner reassuringly, as he too, stopped. "I know", I laughed back. "She's just being friendly . . . ."

It was Edward Seago. I remembered clearly a sketch in one of his books; here the drawing had come vividly to life.

We each murmured something unintelligible; he smiled, and rejoined his companions, and I walked back to the village.

Our meeting was indeed a million-to-one chance, and the incident was over in less time than it takes to tell, yet nothing could have given me greater pleasure than that chance encounter, one happy day in Ludham.

(* Robert Bridges "I love all Beauteous Things".)

"MRS. SAM"

She used to climb our garden path,
(And shocking steep it was,)
Sort out the letters, smile, and say
"Them's yours m'dear" - without a pause,
    Did Mrs. Sam.

It didn't matter, rain or shine,
Her smile was just as bright;
A rosy face, and twinkling eye,
And uniform - a bit too tight,
    Had Mrs. Sam.

When first I knew her, I supposed
Her shortened name to be
A reference to her husband, or
That her initials were the key,
    Like Mrs. S.A.M.

But no, it wasn't long until
The mystery was cleared;
For close at heel a spotted dog
(Dalmation breed) which now appeared,
    Was Sam.

Sam took his duties seriously,
I never knew him shirk;
He carried parcels, opened gates,
And guarded mail - he loved the work
    Did Sam.

There's new ones on the job today,
It's just become "the post",
And as I take the letters in
I don't know which I miss the most, ·
    Mrs. Sam, - or Sam.

"FLORAL FIREWORKS"

"FLORAL FIREWORKS"

We had just finished the last of the rum butter, to my great regret. It was one of the products we always liked to buy at the Flower Show, and it is still linked in my mind with lavender, pot pourri, honey, and ripe peaches, these being other items we often purchased there, too.

I like to remember the Shrewsbury Floral Fete in the mid forties/fifties period when, after the War, people were eager for such peaceful pleasures, and before commercial competitiveness gained too strong a hold. In those days, the spectacle of sun-ripened grapes and peaches, rosy apples and golden pears, monumental displays of vegetables, and honey of every kind and colour, was still a matter for wonderment. The days of rationing were a recent experience, and such glimpses of returning prosperity were mouth-watering indeed.

At that time we lived near the Showground, and it was possible to go in quite early to see the Big Tent, (always referred to in that way.)   This was the principal feature; within it were staged all the largest and most spectacular displays.

Down the first avenue one passed the mammoth stands of the large Nursery and Seed firms;   then on to smaller "specialist" ones showing carnations, chrysanthemums, sweet peas or dahlias.   There was a firm specialising in roses, including miniature ones, which was always a great attraction.   Another section was devoted to a laid-out garden, cleverly contriving a natural effect, with a stream of running water, sometimes a lily pool, a bridge, or a rock garden.   One year, I remember, the stream actually had live fish in it - a touch of realism which younger visitors did not fail to appreciate.

Turning a corner there were the "mixed display" stands, their continuous lines forming breathtaking herbaceous borders.   Here one could find "set pieces" too, composed entirely of flowers, such as a book, animal, butterfly, or toy; in fact any object that would lend itself to being so reproduced.   I remember seeing a child's cot, the tall headboard draped in frills, with a white pillow, blue coverlet, and the white sheet turned down over the top . . . . and all these effects had been achieved solely with flowers.

13

Then - perhaps the most appealing of all - came the Alpine section, with all the charm of Lilliput.   Gentians, dianthus, campanulas, saxifrages, and a whole host of others - only a few inches high, bloomed happily among rock crevices or spilled over stones and walls, according to their habit, while miniature conifer trees, no more than a foot tall, provided an effective contrast.   Here there was invariably some delay, while we members of the public, like so many Gullivers, leaned over to admire and exclaim at them all.

Once having explored the Big Tent, a diversity of other attractions offered themselves.

The musically inclined could listen to selections played by famous Regimental massed bands, and rest their aching feet at the same time; others preferred to watch the juggling and balancing acts on the open-air stage, or thrill to the suspense of the high trapeze act.   Sometimes too, there would be a gymkhana event, or a display by Army or Police Force motor cycle riders.   And of course, there were still the other tents and booths to see . . . .

My own choice was usually the Cottagers' Tent.   It was less grand than the Big Tent, but full of interest in many ways.   I liked to study the many and varied entries in the "Table Decoration" section, and ponder whether the judging agreed with my own.   This applied to the wedding bouquets, too; each set styled for a bride and two attendants.

There was a beautiful display of miniature arrangements, (one I especially admired, in a silver thimble.)   They were masterpieces of skill and ingenuity, and I thought what patience it must have needed to produce each one.

"A container of mixed flowers".   Here was a challenge to any amateur, and the response was always enthusiastic.   So too, were the entrants for various classes such as "Ten carnations" (or roses, dahlias, etc.) or a plate of "Eight dessert apples" (or tomatoes, onions, potatoes, runner beans, etc.)   Plate after plate, and row after row, testified to the fact that we are indeed a nation of gardeners.   Being a very indifferent vegetable grower myself, I gazed with envy upon such achievement.

Few people, I think, would leave without seeing the Honey Section.   Here was mystery indeed.   It was usually draped round with canvas screens, from behind which came a continuous drone - mostly conversational, with the bees contributing a lower-toned accompaniament.   This was obviously territory for experts.   Here were gathered solemn-faced gentlemen who circulated among and around the exhibits of bees and honeycombs like so many outsize bumblebees themselves.   It all seemed dark, warm and rather dangerous, and it was a relief to find a way through to a somewhat lighter and more feminine atmosphere. This was where the different kinds of honey were displayed, together with cakes, scones, biscuits and other delicacies to demonstrate the various uses that could be made of it. After the cave of bumblebees it was heartening, and I felt that bees should certainly be tolerated, if not understood.

A day at the Flower Show must have been a long and tiring one for those visitors who came early and stayed right through until the firework display at night. The Show always takes place in August, and at that time of year it is usually dark enough by half past nine for the display to begin. Erected on stands along the river bank, and augmented with a good variety of rockets, star showers and the like, they made a spectacular grand finale to the day.

This particular year I had not gone to the Show, due - among other things - to moving house. Consequently, we also had a new garden. It was a well planted and established one, but it would be some time before all the plants and shrubs it contained had introduced themselves to us for the first time.

One sunny day in September, when it was far too hot to do any work in the garden, I was wandering round looking for any newcomers, when I found, half hidden under a hedge, some straggling flowers I had not seen before. It transpired they were heleniums, of a brilliant flame colour with strikingly dark centres. They reminded me of something . . . I wandered on and found some sprays of montbretia — it went with them rather well, and some small pink and gold chrysanthemums.

It was while I was putting them in water that I remembered. Fireworks - of course! They looked just like the ones we called "Catherine wheels", and their curved stems and distorted shapes added to the resemblance. And the orange, star-shaped montbretia flowers were very like the outbursts of stars from a rocket firework. The chrysanthemums, too, added light and colour to the general effect.

They were interesting to paint, and with a background of dark blue, like the August night sky, I felt the finished picture could well be called "Floral Fireworks".

And the little figure? A Spanish orange-seller, made of shells. She seems to be watching the fireworks, as I have done so often; - and so, perhaps, have you.

"A VISIT TO LUDLOW"

A hoary old town, perched all of a heap
  Round the hill with the Castle crown;
But there's never a place to weary your feet
  Like Ludlow, Up-and-Down.

Climb up to the Castle, recalling the past
  And history's deeds of renown;
While the tower can give you the best view of all
  Over Ludlow, Up-and-Down.

Stroll down to the river, by Dinham, perhaps,
  For here is no furrow or frown;
No pleasanter spot, - but you have to climb back
  Into Ludlow, Up-and-Down.

In Autumn, the Whitcliffe is spangled with gold,
  The Clee Hills, a warm russet brown;
And the Teme is a ribbon of silver, which weaves
  Round Ludlow, Up-and-Down.

It may weary the feet, but it gladdens the heart,
  That lovely and friendly old town;
I've a note in my diary; back there next year
  To Ludlow, Up-and-Down.

"IN MUCH WENLOCK"

We all assembled, nervously, on the Friday evening. At least, I was nervous.   Some of the others were too, I think, although the more advanced and professional members of our local Art Society were quite relaxed and at ease. They knew the programme and what to expect, as well as having greater confidence in their own abilities than we mere amateurs had.

We crowded together into the rather small studio, jostling against the rows of chairs placed there in readiness.

"Hello, Mary . . . I am glad you could come". "Evening, Mr. Smith.   I did like the woodland one you did last time, did you finish it?"

"Oh, I scrapped mine - I tried to do a figure, and of course that messed it up."

"You sit here, Nora, you'll hear better in front . . . ." and so on.

Finally we are settled, and observe that the tutor has already come in and is chatting unobtrusively to one or two senior members.   Someone says "Shush!" and everyone "shushes" everyone else in sibilant whispers.   Silence, and an air of expectancy similar to that which precedes a conjuror, fills the room.

Our tutor on this occasion, a quiet and unassuming person, welcomes us with an informal talk on the pleasures of outdoor sketching, interspersed with a few amusing anecdotes against himself, and we are soon completely at ease, and fascinated by the demonstration in painting which he now gives us, on a sheet of paper pinned to a blackboard.

In little more than two hours he has produced a picture, and we have learned a great deal.   So much that we are almost bursting with it, and long to find release in trying to paint a picture too.

And that is just what we are going to do, tomorrow.

We reassemble next morning, prepared for battle.   Well, not exactly, though from the strange and varied gear in evidence, one might be excused for thinking so.   There are easels, sketching boxes, tripods, collapsible chairs, folding stools, bags, haversacks, and jars and boxes galore.   With one moderate-sized haversack I feel meagrely equipped, until I remember that an oil painter's kit is necessarily larger and more bulky than for watercolour.

Members with cars have obligingly given lifts to those without (I come in the latter category), and we have just been decanted, a straggly group, in the picturesque old Shropshire town of Much Wenlock.

"IN MUCH WENLOCK"

There are beautiful old buildings - the ancient Guild-hall, a row of timbered cottages, a mellowed stone Church, and of course, the wonderful ruins of St. Milburga's Priory. There is so much - we are spoilt for choice!   Our tutor wisely restrains us from tackling the most formidable and difficult things first, and suggests a number of less ambitious subjects.

Someone settles at once for a black and white cottage tucked in a corner near the Church; another for a glorious chestnut tree shading the green.   We break up into small groups and finally wander off alone.

In the Priory grounds I find Mr. Smith making a commendable sketch of a Norman archway; Mary waves to me from the cloisters garden.   I walk away rather guiltily -

nearly everyone has started work, and still I am undecided. In desperation I plunge into the churchyard - perhaps round that corner of the church. . .? Not bad, but I can't get a good composition . . . . Oh, why didn't I stay at the Priory? Just as I turn to go, the tutor materialises quietly beside me.

"Yes, I think that would be a pleasant group - the tall tombstone to the left, and the cottages round there, and the tree a little off centre - I should try it out."

I will try it out - anything to break the spell and get started. Absurd to feel so panicky. Just unfold your stool, find sketching block, pencil and rubber, paints, brushes and water jar. Ah, that's better. When sitting down, and viewed through the periscope of my cupped hands, it is rather nice.

Time passes, amazingly quickly. We break for lunch, cramped and hungry, yet reluctant to stop. All too soon it is late afternoon, and time to leave.

Arrangements are made for meeting tomorrow. Has anyone heard the weather forecast? "Yes - fine in the morning; rain spreading from the west later in the day." It is only too familiar. "Better try to get here as early as possible, in case they're right."

Sunday morning finds us back in Much Wenlock, eager to begin work, and with an anxious eye on the (so far) unclouded sky.

Throughout both days, the tutor visits each of us in turn, to give advice, criticism and encouragement as and when it is needed.

"Yes, the grouping is all right, and I like your colouring. That tone needs to be darker; study the shadows more. That doorway isn't quite right - more like this," and quickly he shows me how, on the back of his notebook. Magically it begins to look better. If only I could work faster! Some of the members, I know, have produced two pictures in the two days. I envy them their skill, and work on.

The doorway is better, but the tree isn't right yet; and those shadows . . . what shadows? There aren't any; at least, everything now seems to be in shadow, and even as I look up raindrops spatter on the tin lid of my paintbox. Just time to wrap up the picture, the paints and myself, before it is raining hard.

Looking rather like refugees from a science fiction film, we make our way back to the cars, pile in, and lose no time in getting back to town for the most important part is still to come.

By 7 p.m. (fed, tidied and rather out of breath) we are

all back at the studio.   There is no awkward silence this time - we are all talking twenty to the dozen.

"How did you get on?   Let me see . . . hm, very nice." "Have you seen Joan's - hers is lovely."   "Mr. R. has done two . . ."

We chatter on, while all paintings are laid down on a table, ready for the tutor's criticism.

A large easel stands across the corner facing us, adjusted to get the maximum light. Each painting in turn is displayed, and its' merits and faults examined and discussed.   It is all informal and greatly interesting, the pang of failure and the glow of success are shared by us all, and we assimilate a good deal of helpful information while waiting, with mixed feelings, for our own painting to emerge from the pile.

Suddenly it does so, and for a fleeting instant appears divorced from oneself, as though seen for the first time. Pleasure or distaste register with the speed of a camera shutter before recognition comes.

It is my own, and to my relief it doesn't compare too badly with some of the others; I feel it could have been quite a bit worse.   It has its full share of criticism, but it achieves some kindly comment, too, and the general feeling is one of friendly encouragement.

The pile on the table gradually lessens, and finally the last one passes to the easel, and so to its owner.

We feel spent, satiated, and content.

I walk home through the wet streets, the picture tucked beneath my arm.   In time it will fade, perhaps be lost, or even thrown away. It does not really matter. The pleasures of painting cannot be described adequately . . . . only experienced.

"WINTER'S CHILD"

A hellebore today I found,
Close to the snow encrusted ground;
From biting winds it turned, as I
To shelter under leafage dry;
Beset with winter, in the earth
Some flowers still must come to birth;
I watch in wonder, hellebore,
Child of winter's bitter core;
In summer fair you lie asleep,
And all your pristine beauty keep
To shed your wraps in winter time:

Yours is a braver heart than mine!

"ON THE BANKS OF THE LYM"

At the time of writing it is December, sharply cold, and with patches of snow already lying on the hills. I draw the curtains against the sombre day, turn gratefully to the warmth and cheer of an open fire, and in imagination it is Maytime, and I am in that corner of Dorset which spills over into Devon.

Lois and I are having breakfast in the little cottage we have rented for a brief holiday. It is a fine clear day, and the sun winks tantalizingly round the corner by the front window. Hastily we share the last piece of toast, and bundle everything else into the tiny kitchen. Time, tide and sunshine wait for no man, and we long to be far afield, lured by the smiling sea, yet equally wooed by the dappled greenery of the countryside.

Sea, or country - which shall it be? I love the sea, but as a summer visitor only it is mainly the charm of novelty. To paint it requires long study, and for this we have no time. The countryside is familiar territory, and offers better scope.

We hurriedly assemble some packed food, collect our painting gear and emerge, rather breathlessly, into the sunny street.

"Where shall we go?" appealed Lois, whose first visit it was. "I think the country would be best; there are some attractive little corners inland, and it isn't very far . . ."

"That counts" said Lois firmly. "It's going to be a very warm day, and this stuff's pretty heavy."

We turned away from the already well populated sea front, and followed the stream which threads its' way through part of the old town, revealing at every turn some quiet beauty. Stone cottages, their gardens brimming with flowers; little houses and shops in happy juxtaposition, which no modern planner would have tolerated; an old Inn, just on a corner where its' inviting sign and slightly tip-tilted angles caught the eye; willows over the stream beside a footbridge, - oh, the pictures were unending, but as so often happens, they were too close to human activity to be paintable without interruption. Gradually these attractions were left behind; the road dwindled to a mere track through open meadows, and only the stream kept us company.

I had recalled the old Mill from a previous visit, and I knew that Lois would enjoy seeing it as much as I had. Our approach was stealthy - almost as though any undue disturbance might cause it to vanish into thin air.

The setting was perfect. It stood in a wide expanse of meadowland, bright with daisies and buttercups. The footpath meandered quietly past, and lost itself in the shrubby rising ground beyond, and the little stream whispered over its' stony bed beside the long garden, and then disappeared from view under the old mill wheel.

Originally perhaps two cottages, the Mill house presented a long frontage of mellowed stone to the southerly view (which was our approach) and a roof of unbelievably smooth, silver thatch. The extensive garden which stretched before it was well planted and cared for, though in simple style, with rows of vegetables and a gay profusion of flowers, but it was the honeysuckle that gave the crowning effect. A low wall beside the front path foamed with it, and the original substance of the hedge was completely hidden under a canopy of golden blossoms. The mill wheel had been covered over with a lean-to of corrugated iron (the only jarring note), but here the honeysuckle had excelled itself, contriving to hide all trace of the humble structure that supported it.

No sound disturbed the stillness; bees murmured along the hedge, and the light chirrupings of birds came and went through the warm air. And we were stilled too, captured by the timeless quality of it all.

"Out of this world" murmured Lois presently.

"Absolutely" I agreed. "Oh - fancy *living* there - waking up to all this . . . wouldn't it be heavenly?"

"I'm not too sure" said Lois the practical. "It could well be damp, and there's probably some woodworm or dry rot, - and can you imagine all the insect life sheltering under that thatch?"

"Don't tell me" I pleaded. "In any case, I should have a bench in the garden, and sit there all day and look at the house."

"That would be the trouble" said Lois, more thoughtfully. "No work would get done. It's too dream-like . . . a bit unreal. But I wouldn't have missed it for anything. What do you think - for painting, I mean?"

I shook my head. Even if we had had time for such a subject, the picture would be of an "olde-worlde" cottage; a hackneyed theme which would fail utterly to convey its' real charm. One cannot paint "atmosphere" in that sense.

We followed the path on through the meadows, across another footbridge, and found the parent stream. It curved and twisted over the rocky bed it had channelled for itself, in the delightful way that rivers do, and we tracked along after it, down a green slope, round a clump of bushes - and there, at last, I found my picture.

Our painting bags slid to the ground almost of their own volition, and with no word spoken, we selected a grassy hollow on the bank, and sank gratefully into it.

"On the banks of the Lym" I said quietly. "And bonny as Loch Lomond" replied Lois. "Just look over there. I've counted almost twenty different flowers, and I'm sure there are lots more. It has a richness that's more like a wild garden than just a natural place. It's fascinating - I could stay here all day."

"That's all right, then" I murmured . . . . "I love that bit - the stream swirling round that tree, and the lovely depths under the bushes this side, and the stones and shallow pools here in front . . . ."

I went down to the edge of the water, found a dry place for my canvas stool, and unpacked my materials. Lois, equally absorbed, went off flower hunting, and I settled down to paint.

"ON THE BANKS OF THE LYM"

24

Oh, - but it was difficult! The scene was enchanting; the sparkling water, the sun-washed stones, the green depths beneath the eroded bank, and the wealth of flowers and ferns which covered every inch round the base of the old tree, - how could all that be conveyed to one small sheet of white paper?

As many children do, I had always loved to take home largesse from any expedition; a few shells from the seashore; nuts from the hedgerow; flowers - bluebells, buttercups or any such kind, from lane or meadow. In the same spirit, I longed to capture this beauty too.

First, I tried a rather timid pencil sketch, with one or two false starts. Then it began to take shape, and I grew more confident. Now, surely, I could start with colour? This is always a great temptation (for me, at least) to use colour too soon, with the mistaken idea that it will be easier and more effective. I remember one tutor saying - "Study your subject for as long as possible, until you have it clear in your mind; mistakes are not easy to put right." What good advice, and how astonishingly difficult to carry out. Each time I vow I will spend longer in studying the subject first, and so often my treacherous hands are busy with a paint-brush, far too soon.

It has happened again, for I have plunged (metaphoric-ally) into the stream, with cobalt blue and cadmium, flowing joyously on to viridian, ultramarine and a touch of raw sienna, when a quiet voice reaches me . . . "Do you feel you could stop for a bite of something?" - and there is Lois, with our lunch tastefully laid out in the green hollow.

The afternoon fled on wings. Lois did some quick sketches from which to build up a picture at home. (She can paint from memory; I, alas, cannot do so.) I struggle on, until the time comes when one stops, quite suddenly, from the sheer inability of eye and brain to direct one's hand. For better, for worse, it is done; the creative urge is spent.

In the evening, fed and rested, I look at my picture again. There are many faults, and I must try and put some of them right, but for all its' imperfections, it is my record of a very happy day. I have brought home my "buttercups" once again.

"A CHILDHOOD MEMORY"

They've felled the trees in Onibury wood,
And it saddened my heart to see
The mightiest forest a child ever knew,
Reduced to the height of my knee.

A wonderful country, as wide as the world,
Lay through the little brown gate;
The path to the hilltop, - to left, or to right,
Which venture, and which one must wait?

A glimmer of primroses, early in Spring
Would lure me away to the right,
And even to trespass - the best ones to reach,
Before wriggling away out of sight.

In Autumn, no question - the track to the left,
Was very rewarding indeed;
With blackberries, beech nuts, and hazel nuts too,
What more could one possibly need?

And once in a while, in the mood to explore,
The path to the quarry I'd tread;
A haunt for hobgoblins and dragons and things
That go "bump" when you're safely in bed.

But the grandest of all was the path up the hill,
To a stile that led straight to the sky;
The stateliest trees lined the way to the top,
Where a glitter of gold met the eye.

All over the meadow the buttercups brimmed,
While perched on the stile top I'd stare;
I like to think now, as it seemed to me then,
That the sun's always shining up there.

" ALL HONESTY"

It was rather a sad occasion, I thought, as I joined the throng of people crowding into the hall where the Auction sale was to be held. It was a country sale, and of a kind which the local people often attended. The contents of several cottages and dwellings were being disposed of, and usually this resulted in a "mixed" sale. Anything might turn up, from a rusty scythe to a Rembrandt. There was always that kind of subdued but hopeful excitement about it.

I had come early, to have a thorough look around. Alas, there were no paintings by Rembrandt, but there were several modest items which I would try and bid for. One especially I liked; a small drinking vessel in green glass. (I believe the type originated in Germany, and are known as "Roemers".) Not only for wine; it could be filled with small flowers - primroses and violets perhaps? A picture was forming in my mind's eye . . . . .

More people were arriving, but it was still early, and I knew that it would be some time before my "Lot numbers" were reached. I looked around for some quiet corner where I could wait in comparative comfort. Half hidden behind a pile of trunks and boxes was an old rocking chair, and this made an ideal refuge.

Now rocking chairs, by their very nature, are apt to lull one into a semi-dreamy state, or even to fall asleep. I must keep awake at all costs. Idly, I turned to a pile of boxes nearby. Books are irresistable, and the first to come to hand was a well-worn cookery one. I scanned the recipes; read the household hints, and even the few advertisements at the end. "Liver and bacon, 7d. per lb. Plaice, 6d." And farther on . . . "Oil lamps, 25 to 100 candle power, 1d. for 100 hours." It made strange reading in the world of today. I pulled out the next book - a Bible, cared for and protected by covers. Inside was the inscription "1st prize for reading, to Sarah Jones, 1883."

I was wide awake now, as I realized where these possessions had come from, and the identity of their owners.

The Miss Joneses of Chelmick . . . . the wheel of memory spun backwards down the years, to sunny days before the War.

"Haven't you ever been there? You *have* missed a treat. There is always such a variety; I don't know how they do it. And their suppers are grand, too, - 'specially after that walk. It's better to let them know in advance if you can . . . . that seems only fair. After all, there's no electricity or anything . . . ."

There certainly wasn't. There were no "mains" services of any kind in that hidden valley in the hills. Instead, water was obtained from a spring, and oil lamps and candles provided illumination at night (though in those days and conditions it was not unusual to go to bed before dark, and rise when the birds' dawn chorus heralded the return of daylight.)

The three sisters had made their home in a tiny cottage, stone built and thatched, and which was almost entirely wrapped in a magnificent cloak of wisteria. Beatrix Potter herself might have conjured it into existence. The door always stood invitingly open, but no visitor was ever permitted to cross the threshold. That, it seemed, was an unwritten law, and one which was duly respected by everyone.

The garden ground was quite extensive, though not laid out in any formal manner, and here again, visitors were not encouraged to explore. There was a very good reason for this; in high summer, the most luscious strawberries and raspberries appeared on the tea table, gathered only a short time before.

From the cottage, a stone flagged path led up a slope to the visitors' tea room. This was a sturdy "summer-house" built of timber, and inside divided to contrive two small side rooms in addition to the main one, which could only just accommodate a dining table and a few chairs, half tucked beneath. There were a few shelves and ledges around the walls, providing space for a variety of photographs and family mementoes.

My first visit there was in pre-war days. Our walk led us up a country lane, over green fields, through a wooded copse and beside a merry little stream, to cross the brow of a hill, and presently to descend into the Chelmick valley. We found the cottage, and rather over-awed by Miss Sarah's dignified manner, asked - "Would it be possible to have tea today, please?" Her reply was a composed "Certainly - it will be ready in half an hour; please come back then." We took the hint, and went for another walk.

On our return, we were shown into the tea-room, sat down on the chairs placed in readiness, and gazed - speechlessly - at the table. Miss Sarah then brought in a tray laden with freshly brewed tea; assured us we could have more if required, and left us to it.

We were ravenously hungry, but even so, it seemed sacrilege to demolish the spread before us. There were wafer thin sandwiches with different fillings, rolls and scones of several kinds, light sponge cakes, portions of rich fruit cake, a kind of shortcake, dainty little confections like miniature meringues, and still others . . . . There were "two of every-thing", and we noticed later that the number of persons in a party governed the number of eatables served on each plate. I seem to remember it was on that occasion I counted no less than fifteen varieties, every one of them a delight. While consuming the feast, we looked out at the tiny cottage, and marvelled how it all could possibly have been done.

It was while we lingered, rested and replete, that we discovered one clue to the puzzle, and on later visits we learned a bit more, albeit very little. In their youth, at least one of the sisters had been trained and worked in the service of an aristocratic family; (it was rumoured, in a Royal household.) We did not care to probe inquisitively among the photographs and souvenirs, but it explained their cookery skill and expertise, and their style of service; disciplined, capable, and with an odd "remoteness" it was difficult to define. By the standards of today everything was against them; no modern equipment or "helps" of any kind; no transport (they walked the steep hill road to town and market, laden with heavy baskets, both ways.) They had produce to sell, and returned with their own needful supplies for the week ahead. And so the years had passed . . . .

A babel of sounds broke into my reverie. People were crowding round me, and not far away a voice was crying "Five pounds for this trivet . . . a real bargain; you don't find these every day . . . Come along now - any advance on five pounds. .?"

The saleroom came into focus again, and would-be buyers pressed closer. One was a young woman wearing the shoulder badge of the Iona Community; nearby were a Canadian couple. Mingling with familiar Shropshire faces there were many strangers too.

"Oh yes - sure I remember . . . St. Dunstans was evacuated here in the war . . . . We used to take folks over there . . . they were tickled pink . . ."

"I used to come in the school holidays; it was worth walking miles for. We had to behave though; they were strict in their way . . ."

"My son is back in Australia now, but he'd love to have a reminder of those days . . ."

The ripples of memory flowed on - out to other scenes and places, and even other countries. My feeling of sadness lifted, for I felt that the days of hard work, struggle and determination were somehow vindicated. Such example would be hard to follow.

The sale went on and in due time I fought for possession of the little green glass, and was able to bring it home in triumph, where by way of celebration, it was put to its' original use.

One fine day however, when flowers were blooming in the garden, I went in search of some to paint. There were plenty to choose from, but mostly of the "tall and straight" variety like daffodils and tulips. I needed something smaller, and simple. In a neglected corner I found a self-sown plant (or a weed?), tall and straight also, but adorned with what looked like bunches of purple violets . . . only later did I realize what it was. Indoors, I experimented with the green glass and the "violets", but something was needed to lighten the effect, to add a little sparkle. I found the answer in the tool shed, where I had unkindly stuffed some of last year's Christmas decorations . . . "Honesty" seed heads. These, as all children know, are the thin silvery discs which remain when the dry outer covering protecting the seeds has been stripped away.

Violet, silver, and green . . . the seed heads of one year, and the flowers of the next.

The Roemer picture was complete, and with thoughts of the Miss Joneses still in my mind, the title "All Honesty" seemed very appropriate.

"ALL HONESTY"

"THE LEVEL CROSSING"

Old Ted, he was the signalman,
When I was young and slim;
And my great ambition was to be
A signalman, like him.

His house on stilts was full of charm,
The contents, even more;
With needles, bells and levers grouped
From ceiling to the floor.

His many functions busied him,
Once "duty" had begun;
The needles shook; the bells rang shrill,
It seemed such lots of fun!

And when a train was signalled near,
He closed the crossing gates;
For goods train slow or fast express,
Road traffic stands and waits.

The years sped on, and now I find,
My outlook has reversed;
I'm one of those who wait for trains
Until we are dispersed.

But never does this trouble me,
And neither you, I trust;
While waiting, say, at Onibury
As well we sometimes must.

I look up at the signal box,
And feel a wistful joy;
I might have moved those gates myself
Had I been born a boy.

"A DAY AT CROMER"

When on holiday, I suppose we all hope optimistically for a period of settled weather, with bright sunny days, warm caressing breezes, and of course, never a spot of rain to dampen either our spirits or our mackintoshes.   But British summer weather is, to put it mildly, very changeable, and is capable of anything from light rain showers to snow, gales, frost, thunder, hail and cloudbursts.

On my holiay in Norfolk it was no exception, and the day I went to Cromer the weather was very changeable indeed.

The day, deceptively, had started well.   It was July, sunny and very warm, and I thought it would be ideal to visit one of the seaside towns.   I chose Cromer, partly on the strength of a friend's description of happy holidays she had spent there in her childhood, and partly because, living far inland, I always looked forward to "a breath of sea air".   On this occasion that wish was certainly granted.

Provided with a packed lunch, thermos, painting materials and a light raincoat, I caught an early bus to the seaside.   Before we reached the coast the sky had clouded over, with little sun, and it was noticeably cooler, and on alighting at the terminus, it seemed that half a gale was blowing.

My recollections of the next hour or so are hazy, and I remember little of the town, or the high cliff walk along the sea front, but only the grey sky and steel grey sea, rain showers, and a biting wind.   John Masefield's lines, "a grey mist on the sea's face", and "a wind like a whetted knife" came into my mind as I stared unbelievingly and with child-like disappointment at that stretch of the Norfolk coast. So this was Cromer, scene of happy holidays, on a warm and sunny July day (at least, inland.)   Here it was blustery, piercingly cold, and looked like mid-November.

I went down on to the beach, in the hope of finding some sheltered spot, but there was none, and feeling more depressed than ever, I walked back up one of the zig-zag paths that led to the cliff top.   At each angle of the path, little shelters had been built (evidently the local Council knew their Cromer!) and I was thankful to reach one of these havens and step into comparative warmth.

"A DAY AT CROMER"

Looking out of my shelter at the wide, empty expanse of sea (while blowing vigorously on my numbed hands) I pondered what and where was the nearest land. Norway? - that was farther east, and Iceland and Greenland would lie more to the west. There was nothing else out there - nothing at all. If you take a line due north from Cromer, you encounter nothing until you reach the Arctic Circle, and finally the North Pole. It made Lands End, facing North America, seem almost cosy by comparison.

My gaze wandered down the path to the next shelter where two women were deep in conversation, their heads nodding and tossing like flowers in a breeze. Their hats added to the illusion. One was a flat white one, with a band of yellow trimming; idly, I christened her Daisy. The other blue, small and close fitting - she should be Bluebell. Daisy was the dominant one. Bluebell listened more than she talked; she was a very attentive listener. Presently Daisy's narrative seemed to reach a climax; her hands were agitated, her mackintosh askew, and the hat tip-tilted over one ear. Bluebell was more composed, but swayed and nodded gently in the wind, climatic and conversational.

In the absence of any other distraction it was entertaining to watch, and I was quite sorry when Daisy got up, shook herself like a terrier coming out of the water, straightened the hat with one well placed slap, and led the way up the slope with Bluebell meekly following. The stage was empty again.

I looked at my watch - just after 11 o'clock - and debated whether to return to Norwich. It seemed a defeatist attitude, and I hadn't expected to be back before evening. In any event, it was too late to make alternative plans - nearly half the day had gone already; I wished heartily I had not come. There were no painting prospects either, which was a keen disappointment, for to me that was part of the pleasure.

Cold and miserable, I stared at the shelter below me, and the distant beach. Hopeless - the best that could be said for it was that it offered a good study in perspective drawing. Hm . . . . might as well kill time that way as any other, and my abilities with perspective left a lot to be desired. I dragged out my sketching block and pencil and started working it out. Fix the horizon line, and avoid dead centre. The shelter was tricky, it was nearly a bird's eye view. No, that wouldn't do. I rubbed it all out and started again . . . .

When I next looked at my watch it was past two; the sun had made a tardy appearance, and the whole coastline had a warmer light.   Even the sea, though hazy, had a touch of blue.

Like a dormouse emerging from its' winter sleep, I uncoiled sufficiently to find my sandwiches and hot coffee. Ah, that was better!   And though the sun did not add one degree to the temperature, it did enliven the view.   As I looked, two people came up the path and into the distant shelter;   an elderly slender woman, and a crippled boy about fourteen, with one leg in an iron support.

Gradually a picture began to take shape.   The steep bank above the retaining wall was thick with tussocky grass and a few seedling wild flowers, and beyond, the line of high grass-topped cliffs looked golden in the pale sunshine.

I grabbed my paintbox and set to work with all possible speed.   The wall was concrete, solid and grey, but it made a pleasant foil for the grass and yellow stonecrop on the bank. The golden cliffs were lovely, and the sea the colour of a dove's wing, darkening towards the skyline.   White railings marched down to the glass-sided shelter and its' two shadowy figures, and the dark roof gave point to the whole scene.   It was as though someone had switched on concealed lighting over a darkened stage, and everything was bathed in a glow of diffused light.

It was too good to last, and in an hour the sun withdrew; the brief Arctic summer was over.

Back in Norwich that evening, I did full justice to the appetizing meal my landlady had provided.

"I hesitated whether to do a cooked dinner for you today, it's been so very warm" she said, as she placed several piping hot dishes before me, "but I expect it would be a bit cooler by the sea."

I solemnly agreed that it had been a bit cooler there, and then showed her my picture.

"Oh yes, that's Cromer" she said, "but I'd never have thought of painting one of those shelters.   It's surprising, isn't it?   But I'm glad you had such a nice day."

"THE ONNY BROOK"

The memory of that Shropshire stream
From childhood's sunny days,
Returns to haunt me latterly
In quiet and wistful ways.

Its' banks kept guard a thousand things
That gave themselves to me;
It seemed a kingdom set apart
To which I held the key.

Across that chuckling waterway,
A tree had curved its' bole,
And from it, deep below I'd watch
Fat minnows, by the shoal.

And sometimes, on a rustly day,
I'd wade downstream awhile,
And tickle trout with hopeful ease,
But never match their guile.

In Spring, white violets hid themselves
Beneath a hedgerow there;
And ladysmock and meadowsweet
Lent fragrance to the air.

Upon a rougher patch of ground
Where flowers seldom grew;
Globe thistles reared their prickly heads
In shades of smoky blue.

And if to reach the farther bank
I needed any guide;
Some stepping-stones would help my feet
To gain the other side.

Now if you would such pleasures know,
You have not far to look;
For Shropshire sparkles with such streams
As this, the Onny brook.

"OLD GOLD"

I had gone into the shop for a loaf, some teacakes, and a quarter of ham, and I came out deep in thought concerning flowers and flower arrangements.

It was the poster of course, that did it. Fixed up in the side window, above a basket of fresh baked rolls, it read, "You are cordially invited to a Demonstration in Flower Arranging . . . 7.30 p.m. in the Village Hall."

Although Flower Clubs are currently so popular, I had never watched a demonstration, or indeed, taken much interest in the subject. This had been due partly to lack of opportunity, and partly because I prefer flowers to be very simply arranged, almost as they are gathered. To me the art of the professional flower arranger is too exact a "science" or skill, and what is gained by artistry is at the loss of simple appeal. For display work, and special occasions, the skill of the professional is needed, but at home I like simple things, perhaps because of the mounting complexity in every other sphere of activity.

At this time I had recently returned (rather like Rip van Winkle) to a small country town in Shropshire which I had known from childhood. Despite family anxieties, I was very glad to be living there again, and in my mood of happy homecoming, decided to go to the Demonstration; it was pleasant to have the leisure to do so.

There were, I think, twelve arrangements in all, each one meticulously shown and explained to us. First, a carefully chosen container; then the essential materials for holding flowers in place, and sometimes wiring them for extra support, and the cutting or crushing of stalks, where this was considered necessary.

The preparatory work done, there followed the actual arranging of the flowers, each one being placed to achieve "line" and balance. The results were artistically attractive and satisfyingly professional, yet something in me rebelled. Flowers are one of the loveliest harvests of the earth, part of the bounty of Nature. For their brief span they are living things, and exist in their own right. That was it. I felt they were losing their personalities, being subdued and made subservient to an alien cause. The flowers were secondary; it was the grouping that mattered, and I winced almost with pain when a daffodil's stalk was cut to four inches, in order to fit into a studiously allotted space.

The arrangement I liked best was one of three Arum lilies in a shallow black dish. True, their stems had been cut to give graduated heights, and the surplus pieces used to camouflage the holder, but the flowers held pride of place. The adjective "queenly" suits them well, and here too, their majestic quality was not lessened. To dethrone a queen is no light matter.

I was interested, on a later occasion, to talk to the demonstrator (let us call him Harvey,) for I had been surprised to see a young man in the role of flower arranger. His obvious enthusiasm for the subject was infectious, and we soon found mutual interest, though on some points we had to "agree to differ".

"Flowers arranged for style and effect seem to me too stiff for a picture" I reiterated. "I still think the lily one was the best. I'd love to have painted that. A pity I didn't bring my paints with me!"

This was true, and in fact I had even wondered if I might be allowed to use some of his arrangements for that purpose. But flowers are perishable things, and not easy to transport - it was not a practicable idea. We had been discussing it in his flower shop, and I turned to go, feeling a little dejected, when Harvey evidently took pity on me.

"I could make you up an arrangement to try, if you like" he offered. "It's only my idea, but these make rather a nice subject, and they wouldn't fade, of course," and he produced some dried poppy heads, fir cones and grasses of various kinds.

I liked them, and appreciated his offer, but was doubtful about the result. However, I could but try, and he promised to make it up for me during the next few days. At the end of the week I called, as arranged, to collect my "flower study", and Harvey - looking quite eager to see my reaction - took me in to see it.

I had one look, and words failed me. It certainly was lovely; it was also the most difficult subject I could ever have imagined.

The over-all effect was of "old gold" - there was no other colour. It was almost a monochrome. The arrangement was in an old gilt candlestick, and consisted of dried flower and seed heads, corn, grasses and leaves, all, it seemed, in shades of honey, or bleached straw. Just then a shaft of sunlight fell across it, intensifying the gold, and making fascinating shadow patterns among the poppy heads and grasses.

"OLD GOLD"

40

"Do you like it?" asked Harvey, rather hesitantly.

"I think it's perfectly lovely" I answered, and meant it. "There is harmony about it which I like immensely."

He looked pleased, and then produced a length of straw-coloured hessian fabric, and draped it at the back. "I thought that would make a good background" he said. "A definite colour, green, or red or blue, wouldn't look right at all."

I agreed with him; it wouldn't. But the hessian only added to the almost insuperable difficulties it presented from a painting point of view, and my heart sank. I couldn't do it; it was impossible. It served me right for getting involved in the first place. I should have stayed away from Flower Club professionals, and kept to my own ways.

"I'm glad you like it" Harvey said. "Can you carry it, or shall I bring it round for you?"

I couldn't back out now, after all the trouble he had taken for me. That wasn't possible, either.

"Oh - that's all right, I'll manage" I muttered, and escaped as quickly as I decently could.

At home, with the hessian draped over a chair and the candlestick in front, I spent a wretched afternoon. The material was stiff and not easy to arrange, and although in actuality the flowers showed clearly against it, I didn't know how they could possibly be made to do so on paper. I fiddled about with colour washes in all the shades of "honey gold" I could contrive, and by evening I gave it up, tired, dispirited, and in a distinctly bad temper.

When I opened the sitting room door next morning the sun was streaming in, and my "problem child" had undergone a surprising transformation.

No longer was it one colour - there were dozens! Bright amber glowed on the underside of petals; smoky blue shaded the poppy heads; the fir cones were every shade of brown, and the wheat, barley and oats every shade of yellow. On the left, a withered leaf still showed a ghostly green; another the muted red and purple of its' former glory. A long seed pod, split open, revealed a delicate blue and ivory lining, while bracken, beech masts and even a bulrush, acted as a foil and gave tonal strength to the whole composition. It was a joy to behold, and I set to work with a will.

A few weeks later, finished and framed, I took it along to Harvey's shop.

"I thought you'd like to see it" I told him. "You certainly set me a problem, but I think it's come out all right in the end."

He looked at it silently for some time.

"Do you like it?" I ventured, rather nervously. It was my turn to ask that question now.

"I do, indeed," he answered slowly. "It's exactly what I've always wanted. The fact is, I'd like to keep it . . . . would you allow me to buy it?"

And that, in view of its' joint parentage, seemed a very happy outcome.

" TO CARADOC"

I sing small praise of Wrekin,
(An isolated rock;)
For me the hill I cherish most,
Is lovely, golden Caradoc.

When Time was just a seed-head
On a dandelion clock;
I'd race the others, striving first
To scale the ridge of Caradoc.

With aching limbs and laughter,
Like birds to bough we'd flock;
With friends to share our picnics there,
The conquerors of Caradoc.

About her feet were bluebells,
Windflowers and ladysmock;
A glinting stream, and swathes of green
Adorned the slopes of Caradoc.

Years passed, and we were parted
By toil and tears and shock;
But through it all I could recall
Those happier times on Caradoc.

And now - I journey homeward,
My own door to unlock;
Through weathered storm to quiet calm,
And windows wide to Caradoc.

"THE LIGHT SPOUT"

"THE LIGHT SPOUT"

Forty years on . . . . It was all of that since I first set foot in the Carding Mill Valley, en route for the Light Spout waterfall. Recently I came across a photograph of my mother and I sitting on some rocks just out of splashing distance of the fall; I would be about six years old at the time. And now, I found myself there again.

It was more than twenty years since I had walked that familiar ground, and I set off with mixed feelings. The fact that I was now living in the area still seemed almost unbeliev-able, like a happy dream, but through the dream I was conscious of the sharp pangs of reality. I was alone, with only thoughts and memories to bear me company.

How well I remembered the little footpath along the side of the hill that led down to the floor of the valley. If, when walking along it (carefully!) you watched the opposite hillside, you had the feeling of being airborne - not flying exactly, but not on solid ground, either. I found myself trying it out again, but not for very long. It soon caused giddiness, and suppose I fell over the edge, and rolled down the slope? It would ill become my grey hair and substan-tial figure.

A few minutes' walk brought me into the valley itself, and I crossed the stream by a narrow plank bridge. Just below that spot, long ago, I had found my first water musk, their brilliant yellow trumpets bobbing over the water, and had always looked for them there, like old friends.

I passed a fold in the hills where we had our first out-door picnic, with meat and vegetables cooked in an earthen-ware casserole over a wood fire. How good it had tasted, and how hungry we were in that Stretton air.

Each fold of the hills, the trees and bushes, almost the very stones themselves, revived some half-forgotten memory. A quotation came to mind; "Sermons in stones, books in the running brooks, and good in everything." That summed it up very well.

The farther I went the more I became engulfed in the quiet beauty around me. The blue sky was flecked with high clouds, and in the sunshine the hills were patterned by ever-changing shadows. There had been a good deal of rain

45

in recent weeks, and in the clear air the heather covered slopes were startlingly beautiful, each clump appearing larger and more richly coloured than the one before.

The stream rushed and swirled along, now widening into a small blue lake, only to fling itself through a narrow gorge between the rocks, foam into a miniature cascade, and then, chuckling to itself, start all over again. It was difficult not to chuckle too, so infectious was the sense of joy. Here, at least, one could say, "God's in His heaven, all's right with the world." At least, with this tiny corner of it.

I felt an overwhelming gratitude that such peace and serenity existed, and could still be found in a world that is sometimes hardly recognisable as the one we knew in our younger days.

No motor car could possibly invade this hollow in the hills, though it is unhappily true that they can now reach and travel along the top of the hill range, where I remember only a rough track, and mountain ponies grazing the slopes with nothing more startling than an occasional hiker to disturb them. To an ever increasing extent, it seems, those who go on foot are being driven from the town streets, the open roads, and even the country lanes and byways.

In our ardent pursuit of pleasure we are in grave danger of destroying that very peace and unspoilt beauty which can give us the inner replenishment we need so much - now perhaps more than ever before. "The world is too much with us", and it is getting progressively harder to get away from.

I had reached the waterfall, and crossed over to a likely spot on the left bank where I would be able to sit and paint. An armful of dry heather topped with my raincoat made an adequate seat; a large stone wedged firmly to stop my haversack toppling down the bank, and a flat one to support my water jar. I eased myself down on to my heather cushion, propped my feet against a boulder, and contemplated the Light Spout.

What charm and fascination there is in running water! And this miniature Niagara was giving a splendid display. Channelled through a cleft in the rocks, it emerged in a "spout" of sparkling water, only to break on lower rocks into several smaller ones. Ferns grew happily in the crevices between the glistening stones; green water weed flung swaying emerald tapestries over the wet rock walls, and the sky mirrored its blueness in the pools below me. High on the opposite bank, a gnarled and twisted tree stump had produced fresh young branches which reached out, eagerly it seemed, into the flying spray.

I reached out eagerly, too, for pencil and sketching block, when I suddenly became aware of alien sounds. Looking round, I saw two figures approaching; one was equipped with a transistor radio, and from it came what I can only describe as "jungle" sounds, harsh and tuneless, repeated over and over. On they came, the jangling noise with them, until finally they climbed up the rocks to my right and disappeared over the skyline.

I turned back to the waterfall, but it was some time before my outraged nerves relaxed, and I could regain my former state of harmony. Fortunately for me, the sun continued to shine, and the "aliveness" of the scene was irresistable. Never having tried to paint a waterfall before, it needed all the concentrated effort I could muster.

The water never ceased its' cascade; each second something was happening, and the constant movement held one's gaze like a stage. Nevertheless, after several hours' work, I contrived an interval to stretch my legs, have sandwiches and coffee, and refresh my hands and face in a nearby pool.

The afternoon passed swiftly, and all too soon the sun moved away over the hill. I had most of the detail I needed, and the joy of it - I could come again soon if the picture demanded it, or just for the sheer pleasure of seeing it all again.

Soon I was walking back along the stony path among the heather. As I came down towards the junction with the main valley, I saw a woman sitting alone on the bank above the stream. As I drew level she looked up and smiled.

"What is it like farther on?" she asked.

I described the Light Spout, and as I guessed she had come by motor coach from a Midland town, mentioned also that the path had fallen away in places, and it needed some care to get round.

"It's grand here, isn't it? Nice and quiet. I could do with coming here every week," she said.

May our country places always be "nice and quiet" - waiting, as from time immemorial, to respond to the appeal from our inner consciousness for - what?

In my own case I am not in doubt. But for each of us the quest must be a personal one.

"LOST VOICES"

The still small voices that I used to hear
    Are silent now;
In vain I strive to call them back once more
    Yet know not how.

They spoke of Nature and our heritage
    Of living earth;
Of thankfulness for all the land could give
    Nor any dearth.

They whispered of the joy creation brings
    A human heart;
To make for future ages all our own
    Some tiny part.

They taught compassion and the need for strength
    Against all doubt;
For time is short and for us all the sand
    Runs swiftly out.

They loved the silence and the peace it brings
    The troubled mind;
In solitude and meditation we
    Ourselves may find.

Cacophony of discord, louder yet
    Defeats them now;
Those still small voices I must hear again
    But how, - but how?

"THE ATTIC ROOM"

Lois and I were spending a week's holiday together by the sea in the delightful county of Dorset.

Our time there was all too brief, snatched rather desperately from our respective home cares and commitments. A week of freedom, to do just as we wished, was a rare pleasure. We would walk and talk and paint; never look at a clock, eat when we felt hungry, and go to bed when we were tired. And equally of course, get up when we felt so inclined, without the discipline of timetables and rigid hours. I am a reluctant early riser, and much prefer to begin the day with that gentle stimulant "morning tea", and to reflect upon the choices to be made. The whole day lies ahead; it is almost too good to break into it . . . .

To achieve such freedom, away from home, it is necessary to forego certain other things. We had rented a tiny holiday cottage, and fended for ourselves. Fortunately there was an excellent catering establishment not far away, where we usually went for our main meal, and we provided our own breakfasts and packed food to take out. Such chores as washing up and bed-making depended on the weather. If it was a glorious day, they were left until evening, when our united efforts soon disposed of them.

On this particular day the weather was disappointing, with squally rain showers and a chilly wind. The beds were made, the washing up done, and our painting bags lay, like faithful dogs, on the floor near the door, waiting for action.

From the window I watched the rain spattering in a large puddle. Lois came in through the back door after a hasty look at the sky.

"It's no use waiting - there isn't a break anywhere. It might go on all day. If this is summer, we should have come in November . . . . probably be lovely then . . . ."

We sat and gloomed for a while, and then I remembered the attic bedroom. Depression lifted, and I longed to sneak away there at once, but one cannot desert a friend on such a day. Then I noticed that Lois was sorting through some blank canvases and humming to herself. I recognised the signs.

"Come on - where is it?" I teased. "You're just dying to start something . . . ."

49

She looked apologetic. "Well - it's just the roofs and chimneys from my room, and someone's put three little pots of lobelias on top of a wall out there . . . . they must want to see something growing, I suppose. I'd have to work in the window. If I could move the chest of drawers away from the wall, it would give me enough room, I think . . ."

We rushed happily upstairs. The chest was soon moved away, and Lois wriggled her way round the furniture to the window.

"I'll be in the attic - shout when you're hungry," I called, as I hauled my bag up the second flight of stairs.

The cottage (said to have been a fisherman's originally) consisted of a living room, kitchen, food store, and small bathroom on the ground floor; two bedrooms on the first floor, and above them, reached by an almost perpendicular flight of stairs, was an attic bedroom. This had appealed to me on arrival, but after seeing the stairs and recalling the weight of my luggage, I contented myself with a first floor room. But as a place in which to paint it was ideal, and it provided a challenging subject in itself. Those beams! I liked their strength and shape, but thought they would tax my ability with perspective considerably.

"THE ATTIC ROOM"

50

The room was long and rather narrow, with a window at either end. Walls and roof were lined with hardboard panels, and in one place the space behind the wall panelling had been utilized to form a cupboard. The furniture consisted of a bed, with a feather quilt in faded pink, a small table with drawer and mirror, a chest of drawers, and an old-fashioned cane chair. There was no door, and indeed it seemed unnecessary; those stairs would surely guarantee privacy.

It was simple and quiet, and there was an almost monastic quality about it which I found soothing and satisfying.

As I sat in the old basket chair and looked around me, I wondered why it is we surround ourselves with so many possessions, when our basic needs are few. What human squirrels we are, collecting and hoarding so much, until possessions become a burden, or just a goal in themselves. But unlike the squirrels we have an aesthetic sense too; our yearning for beauty and harmony also needs to be satisfied. Shelter, warmth and food for the body; beauty to sustain the mind and spirit . . . surely that should suffice?

But there are all the outside pressures too. Ambition, competitiveness, fashion, new techniques, status symbols; the feverish self-inflicted condition of "keeping up with the Joneses." Why do we do it, when the essentials for living are ours to accept and enjoy? We seem to find it so difficult to streamline our lives, and to savour the simple pleasures of life. The materialistic world displays its' ever-changing wares before us, and all too often we gobble them up, and ask for more. Perhaps we should try harder, each of us, to withdraw a little before we become engulfed, and our inner senses atrophy from lack of use.

The room was quiet and still, and pale sunshine was stealing in through the farther window. And at that moment, sounds floated up the stairs . . . .

"I don't want to disturb you, but I've made some tea. It's good to have a break, one gets so cramped. Would you like a cup?" - and Lois's head appeared above the stair opening.

Willingly I agreed, surrendered the chair to her, and sat on the floor beside it. Presently she glanced in a puzzled way at my blank sketching block.

"I just couldn't get started" I told her. "There's such a restful, withdrawn sort of feeling up here. It's like a sanctuary. One just wants to meditate, thankfully, and to get lost in it. Isn't it odd what an atmosphere some places have?"

"It may be the beams" said Lois, "or perhaps he was a very saintly fisherman. More tea?"

"No, thanks. I'd like to do a painting of it if I can. It would be a keepsake. How are the lobelias, by the way?"

"Oh, not too bad, but the roofs are a problem . . ."

We parted, and I wrestled with perspective until lunch time. It was pleasant then to go for a brisk walk along the sea front, before tucking in to a good lunch which we had not prepared ourselves.

Invigorated and refreshed, we made our way back to the cottage, both of us eager to make the most of the afternoon light.

The ensuing hours ran away like sand through an hour-glass; the attic beams merged together in shadow, and painting time was over.

I eased my cramped limbs out of the chair, (how inviting that bed looked!) yawned widely, and went to look for Lois.

She was busy clearing up, and her picture was on an easel by the window.

"Oh, I *do* like that" I cried, - and I truly did. Between high walls was a glimpse of a little stone house with blue shutters across the street; the foreground was mostly roofs and chimneys, but on top of a nearby wall were the three lobelias - summer blue against the surrounding brickwork.

Late that evening, tired but happy, we looked at our handiwork again. I propped mine in front of the clock on the mantelpiece in the living room, and Lois's larger one occupied a chair across the corner.

"What a place to put lobelias" said Lois, who is a keen gardener. "It wouldn't be too difficult to make a little garden here - tiny rockery perhaps, with alpine plants . . . there's plenty of stone to use. How I'd love to do it. No-one should be without a garden - they miss so much."

"That applies to the attic too, in a way," I agreed. "What a difference it would make if everyone could have a little private retreat; a sanctuary like that where they could escape from all the demands and pressures, and just "be themselves" for a time. To get away from it all - it's the best tonic in the world . . ."

"Yes, I agree" said Lois. "That - and a garden. What strange planners we'd make. I wonder if anyone would agree with us?"

"STEP-A-SIDE"

A funny name to give a place,
But "Step-a-Side" it be;
I reckon it from childhood days,
And it always tickled me.

I had a mind, in those brave times
To step ahead, and far;
For all the world seemed bright with hope,
And a step could reach a star.

'Tis quite a while since that young dream,
And stars stay out of reach;
Ambitions fail, I was to learn,
For the world has much to teach.

I wonder where it all went wrong,
I had no signpost's guide;
'Twould wiser been, I feel small doubt,
To just have stepped aside.

There's comfort in the lanes one knew,
And wisdom there, beside;
When all my striving's done, I'll turn
To home, to Step-a-Side.

"HAWKSTONE MILL"

"HAWKSTONE MILL"

One Friday evening, as so often before, I scanned in a local paper the lists of property for sale. In past years this had been a constant procedure, to try and find a suitable house at a price I could afford. Happily circumstances were easier now, but the habit still persisted.

Near the bottom of the list, in small type, was the following:-

"In isolated position, at northern end of lake, windmill and cottage, in need of considerable repair. Ideal for country retreat. Open to offers."

Despite the wintry end of January, this was irresistible.

"Isolated"? . . splendid. Everywhere was far too crowded nowadays. "A lake" - how romantic that sounded . . . one didn't have the chance of living on the shores of a lake every day. A windmill, too - an unusual feature, and very picturesque. Visions of paintings by famous Dutch artists floated before me.

"In need of repair" and "open to offers" were perhaps the most appealing phrases of all. Because it was isolated, no-one wanted it. Alone and deserted, it was waiting to be re-discovered. Lived in and cared for, it could become a real home once more. Money would need to be spent on repairs, it seemed, but perhaps a modest sum would buy it? On my next free day I would explore.

The day dawned cloudy, brightening occasionally with pale wintry sunshine. Well wrapped up against the cold, I took vacuum flask and sandwiches for my mid-day meal, and also watercolour paints, for I might possibly be able to do some sketching there.

A bus journey and then ten minutes walking found me in a rough country lane, bordering Hawkstone Park. The lane meandered on, round another bend and I followed it, on and on. The surface deteriorated. It was now only a cart track, deeply rutted. I slithered from one side to the other, avoiding the ruts and pools of water with difficulty. How much farther, I wondered? Surely I should be able to see the windmill by now. Then, through the trees and bushes that bordered the path, I saw the solidity of a building. Excitement mounted and I splashed on. Only about fifty yards to go . . . one final slither and a leap for the hedge bank by a gate, and I was there.

And there too, was the cottage. It faced the way I had come, and was separated from the windmill by about a hundred yards of what had once been a garden. There they stood, the cottage and the windmill, and I stumbled about, trying to decide which to explore first.

The windmill had no sails and the gear which had once operated them presented a silhouette of broken shafts and wheels against the cloud-driven sky. A dramatic effect, and interesting to paint; I would try while the weather was fine!

But oh . . . I must see the cottage - and where was the lake? To return home without having seen it was unthinkable, so I set off hastily in search.

For the first time I realized how low-lying the lane was; the hedge bank on the farther side was steep, and overhung with trees and bushes growing along the top. I clambered up the bank and through the edging of trees, and was only just in time to see the gleam of water. I had certainly found some part of the lake, and narrowly missed falling in.

It was more like a river at this point; a stone tossed over would have landed on the opposite bank, but from the map I knew it widened out farther on, though not to any great extent. For about two miles it curved to form a natural boundary round the northern side of Hawkstone Park.

I made my way cautiously back to the cottage, and in a fever of anxiety lest the day be gone too soon, I turned my back resolutely on further exploration, and settled down to paint the windmill.

It was not an easy subject to capture on paper, yet I longed to do so. The sky was good, varied with scudding clouds. Against it, the outlines of the windmill were stark and strong, and its' crown of broken timbers moved me strangely. Perhaps this was due to its' impressive structure, all the work of men's hands, and now abandoned. Almost invested with human personality, it faced desertion and decay with a proud indifference.

Around it lay the semblance of what had once been a garden. There were apple and other fruit trees and bushes, that even now were struggling to survive and yield a harvest again. The prickly strands of brambles and wild roses had penetrated everywhere, only to be partially concealed under the tall rank grass. Here and there I had discovered generous clumps of snowdrops, already in flower. Long stemmed and lovely, they alone were untroubled by human neglect.

Time was passing all too quickly; heavy clouds had gathered and I felt the first ominous spots of rain. Reluctantly, I gathered up my tackle and sought shelter in the cottage.

The key from the house agents was not needed, for they had already warned me of the conditions I would find. Here was desolation indeed. Windows and fireplaces had been ripped out, leaving broken frames and gaping holes. The upper floor had collapsed; one corner rested on the ground, while part of it, round the stairs, was still up, tilted at an acute angle. I crept cautiously inside, testing the structure as I went, but alarming as it looked, it was wedged securely. The area of the living room fireplace, and the angle of the stairs, still in place, afforded the best protection. I hung my raincoat on a handy nail, propped the picture on a pile of bricks, and laid out my lunch on the stairs.

The sagging ceiling gave to this part of the cottage a suggestion of cosiness and warmth. A stout beam still supported the brickwork above the fireplace; there was room for a chimney-seat to be built on each side . . . a wall over there would provide an entrance way and give access to the smaller room at the side.

That door beyond the stairs - was it the back door? No - I opened it carefully, - here was the kitchen. A good size too, with a window looking over rolling green meadowland. True, the roof was open to the sky in places, and long tentacles of ivy wound themselves round the boiler chimney. A timber strut protruded from the wall - a shelf had once been fixed there. I fetched my picture and propped it on the ledge, walked over to the corner by the boiler and in imagination surveyed my kitchen . . . .

It was all there, sound and sparkling, down to the last pot and pan. The shelf was replaced and cupboards added, a cooker beneath, sink and drainers under the window, the view framed in yellow curtains, like sunshine . . . .

Why - it *was* sunshine! The sky was light again, with even a small patch of blue. The kitchen mirage vanished as I hurried out to start painting again.

Hours passed like minutes, in happy concentration. The sunlight emphasised the dramatic effect of the broken winding gear, the strength and rigid outlines of the mill, and even the tangle of vegetation around it. But all too soon the light faded; it was past four o'clock, and painting time was over.

On leaving, I closed the cottage door behind me - a pointless but instinctive gesture. I was grateful for its' shelter and I left it as a friend. The garden path, still faintly defined under so many seasons' growth, led me towards the windmill and the lane.

Some weeks later I heard that the property had been sold, but my curiosity is spent; I shall not visit it again. I witnessed its' last days of impressive dignity, alone on a winter's day, and that is how I like to remember it.

"THE COUNTRY-LOVER"

There are no street lamps in the countryside:
 - but snowdrops glisten where the beech leaves died.

A pavement's clean and level to one's feet:
 - I miss the scent of earth, rain-washed and sweet.

The crowds are thronging, and the shops are bright:
 - the orchard daffodils are my delight.

There's entertainment, dancing, or a show:
 - I'd miss them all, to watch the sunset's glow.

Have you no urge for "Life" - the zest it brings?
 - in solitude, I'm near all living things.

Be buried then, for progress knows no bar:
 - it may be, friend, we have progressed too far.

"OVER THE LONGMYND"

It was Bank Holiday time, yet my country walk was almost deserted, and wonderfully quiet. The weather was dry and reasonably mild for Easter, with pale sunshine and a light breeze. I climbed up the rough hill road, walking at times on grass and among heather. Occasionally the sound of human feet on the stony ground disturbed a number of hill ponies grazing on the slopes nearby; they neighed indignantly and scattered in brief alarm, but soon returned and resumed their feeding. One or two hikers, more energetic than I, overtook me and were soon lost to view along the winding road ahead.

At length I came out on to the hill plateau, to feel the kind of exhilaration and freedom which perhaps winged creatures do on emergence from the chrysalis.

Alas, - this was not last week, or last year. It was an Easter Bank holiday in the nineteen thirties, and I was walking up the Burway and over the hill to the Longmynd Gliding Club. I had never been there before, although I had often watched the gliders in the air, and longed to be in one, floating soundlessly over the familiar Shropshire countryside. I had been told that the Club at that time possessed a dual-seat trainer in which, given favourable conditions and a westerly wind, one passenger at a time could be taken up for a flight.

With the opportunity of a Bank Holiday, - clear settled weather, and a breeze which I was convinced was westerly - surely the day of my first flight had really arrived?

From the Portway, the Gliding Club buildings came into view, which I seem to remember consisted of a large hangar and a small office building, constructed of that serviceable but unlovely material, corrugated iron.

I watched, high above, two or three machines rising and falling alternately, as the thermal air currents carried them. "Machines" is a misnomer, for it was hard to believe that these graceful, gossamer creations could possibly be man made. Even at closer inspection on the ground, they looked frail, unearthly things, of a glistening honey colour, with a small slender body and very long (or should it be wide?) shaped wings. That small body worried me - I hadn't expected it to be quite as small as that, and could only hope that the two-seater would be a more substantial affair.

Meantime, it was very interesting (but a little unnerving) to watch the launching of a glider into the air. Although some distance away, I could see that a tow rope was attached to the nose and then passed to a winch on a motor car. At an agreed moment, the car was driven forward into wind; the glider swished over the grass, and suddenly was catapulted high into the air, and in no time at all had faded to a thin line of gold in the sky. The falling of the tow-rope back to earth seemed the only evidence of it ever having existed.

A friend had joined me for this holiday trek, and together we wandered around the Club buildings and the heather covered ground nearby, looking hopefully for the dual-seat "trainer". An inspection of this wonder, while it was still on the ground, we felt to be desirable. In search of guidance, we gradually edged nearer a small group of people clustered round several gliders in the main launching space. There were some obvious Club members, (we recognised the chief engineer by sight) and a sprinkling of ordinary visitors like ourselves. Presently the group broke up, and the engineer and one or two others moved across to an immaculate glider nearby, waiting ready for take-off.

Suddenly, one of the figures, bare-headed and warmly wrapped in a camel coat and woollen scarf, chanced to turn in our direction.

Incredulously, we recognised Amy Johnson.

The glider we had admired was hers, and later we learned she had come to spend a quiet gliding weekend at the Longmynd Club.

Presently the little knot of people broke up; the famous airwoman disappeared, and clearly - as there would be no public "joy-rides" that day, - we reluctantly decided to set off for home. The exciting moment was over, and we should not see her again.

A few cars, filled with Club personnel, were starting to move. And there - a few yards from us, with hair blowing in the wind, Amy Johnson was beside the open door of her car, about to step in. Fortunately I had my camera, and this was the hour!

"Miss Johnson - please - may I take your photograph?" She paused and smiled, faced the camera, then asked - "Did you get it?"

Indeed, I did get it, and I'm happy to have it still.

. . . .

Decades have passed; changes and troubles have come and gone, and Fate is smiling once more. I have a small home of my own at the foot of the Longmynd hills, and recently a new friend paid me a highly disturbing compliment. Her home is known as "The Manor House", tucked in a secluded hamlet below the western slopes of the Longmynd, and she had asked if I would do a painting of it for her.

Of course, it is a pleasure to be asked - a delightful compliment and I began, like Mr. Toad, to swell with self-importance. But I had never attempted a "house portrait" before, and it was a most disturbing prospect. I felt that her faith in me was unjustified, and that the result was bound to be a dismal failure. Weakly, however, I agreed to make the attempt.

We met again to discuss details. She would transport me and my painting gear from my home to hers, and back again, as often as necessary. Two other factors would be needed - free time from my daily employment, and several days of good weather. I duly arranged the first, and could only hope for the second.

The day came, and bright and early so did my friend (let us call her Tracy.) It was a luxury to be able to pile my packed haversack into a car, and be driven effortlessly (on my part) over the Longmynd. Here, the stony path of former times had become a tarmac road. No ponies grazed the slopes, and cyclists and hikers belonged to the past. Now cars pursued each other up the steep and twisting road, until they met others coming down, when it was necessary to manoeuvre into the nearest lay-by, which had been cut into the hillside for that purpose. (These also make very acceptable havens for sheep during the dark hours.)

The weather was faultless, dry and clear, and once we had left the breezy plateau and descended the steep westerly road, it was calm and pleasantly warm. To the north-west lay the Stiperstones range of hills, crowned by the "Devil's Chair" - a dramatic outcrop of jagged rocks, with an atmosphere all its' own. Other hills rose to the west and south, but below us a river valley had created a softer landscape. Two more twists and turns, over a little stone bridge, - and we had arrived at the Manor.

A warm welcome preceded my exploration of the site. The house was close to the road, but the flat parapet of the bridge was about the right distance away, and here I could spread out my materials. Tracy helpfully provided a plump cushion for my comfort, and soon I was able to sit and study my subject.

It was sheer pleasure to be there; the sun warm on my back, birds singing in the trees, a garden bright with flowers, and the chuckle of the river nearby. It was utterly peaceful.

I recalled the words of Jerome in "Three Men in a Boat" - "I like work, it fascinates me . . . . I could sit and look at it for hours. The thought of getting rid of it . . . ."

This certainly would not do. Sooner or later I *had* to get rid of it. A large piece of white paper stared up at me, and I stared back, wondering how or where to start. And then, as though in answer, the front door opened, and Tracy approached, bringing coffee and biscuits. To my great relief, the spell was broken.

The front door; that was it, - the focal point. Work out the scale and the proportions, pencil it in, and work from there. This discovery rivalled Tracy's excellent coffee as just the stimulus I needed.

The hours sped by; there was much to be done, - but "tomorrow is another day", and we made arrangements accordingly.

My second day there was full indeed. Hours of painting and study passed like minutes. About mid-day however, Tracy coaxed me away to see the garden. Her feeling and enthusiasm for flowers and shrubs and garden planning was infectious, and something I could share and enjoy to the full.

Refreshed and happy, I returned to my perch on the bridge, and worked with a will. All too soon, the sun retired behind the hills, and it was time to pack up and retire too.

Indoors, to my surprise and pleasure, I was invited to join the family for dinner, and a very delicious one it was. (Not least of her talents, Tracy is a "cordon bleu" cook.) By comparison with that distinction, I can do little more than boil an egg, but my appreciation, after a long day in the open air, was unbounded.

We lingered late, and when we finally left for home, stars were twinkling in the night sky. Our drive back over the Longmynd was a very different experience from that of the morning. There were strange distorted shapes; sinister rustling sounds, and glistening eyes that watched us as we passed . . . . ("Drivers should always take care, because of the sheep" murmured Tracy.)

The road curved and dipped, and soon clusters of brighter lights pin-pointed our little town in the valley below. After such a happy day, - what a lovely way to come home!

"STRETTON HILLS"

The Stretton hills have a charm for me,
Whatever the time of year;
From Springtime's greenness to Autumn's gold,
Or when Winter's snows are near.

In sheltered valleys the year's first flowers,
Shine beneath hedgerows bare;
While later, the woods by Caradoc swim
With a million bluebells there.

'Tis said that Summer's the best of all,
And indeed, there is little doubt;
You can hardly better a picnic lunch
Up by the old Light Spout.

The Longmynd's glory is Autumn time,
When the bracken turns to gold;
And wimberry pickers homeward wend,
With all their baskets can hold.

In Winter, with fir trees against the snow,
It is easy to understand
Why Stretton hills should remind us most
Of a miniature Switzerland.

Among those hills, in the rain or sun,
I am well content to roam;
They're lovelier now than they've ever been,
For these are the hills of home.